Ready to Turn Your Idea into a Real Business?

Becoming an entrepreneur is a chance to get creative and help others. It's also a chance to apply all the stuff you've learned in school like math, reading, writing, science, history and art!

But making a business is complicated. It's hard. And it involves hard work. So this Workbook, from the folks who created Lemonade Alley, is here to help you with the many details that make up a great business.

What's Lemonade Alley? It's the kid-biz contest where teams of K-12 kids create recipes, build lemonade stands and sell lemonade to see who can make the most for the charity of their choice. If you'd like to start a Lemonade Alley contest in your neighborhood or school, see lemonadealley.com.

Steve Sue

Chief Lemon Head, Lemonade Alley

LemonadeAlley.com | BizGym.org

© 2015, BizGym Foundation, a 501C3 nonprofit. All Rights Reserved. | Edition 09.14.15

Everything You Need
To Create an Awesome Kid-Biz!

Name your business:

Describe your business idea:

_____

_____

_____

_____

_____

_____

_____

Your business name should be fun to attract customers.

Making your business fun helps people remember and pass on your business story.

Name your main product here:

Product Picture:

Materials Needed:

Journals x50

Scrapbook paper

Adhesive

Ruler

Scissors

Pencil

Your Product can also be a service like helping people do things.

Show how your product will be packaged & presented:

Make sure your packaging makes it obvious what you're selling. Also be sure to put a price on it!

Try to show how to use the product, what it's good for or why it's great.

List extra products you'll sell here:

Product Picture:

Materials Needed:

Additional products are a good way to make more money.

Extra products that are related to main products usually sell better.

List products & include prices:

Our Menu

Make your menu on letter size paper and display on your table. Or make a big overhead menu so people can see it from far away before ordering.

6. Food Safety (for food sellers only)

Food Safety Test:

1. Food and drinks for sale must be made and served according to health laws.

   YES or NO

2. Food and drinks made with heat (stoves, ovens, etc.) must be made and packaged in a certified commercial kitchen like a restaurant.

   YES or NO

3. Pre-packaged food products can be sold if stored properly.

   YES or NO

4. Hand gloves must be used at all times when preparing and serving food and drinks.

   YES or NO

5. Always wash hands and ingredients before handling or cutting.

   YES or NO

6. If you leave your food making area, you must wash your hands again before preparing or serving.

   YES or NO

7. Keep all perishables in food-safe containers like coolers.

   YES or NO

8. Never taste directly from serving tools or storage containers.

   YES or NO

9. Excess liquids and ice cannot be dumped outside and instead must be taken home for disposal.

   YES or NO

10. Animals and pets are not allowed when making or selling food and beverages.

    YES or NO

Always check local health, business and other government laws for latest requirements.

Answers: They're all "Yes"!

List 3 types of customers:

Customer Pictures: **Describe them** (ages & interests):

_____

_____

_____

_____

_____

_____

_____

_____

_____

Pictures help you understand your customers better.

Knowing what people like helps you make things they want or need.

Name your team members:

President:

Your President is the leader and a main salesperson.

Treasurer:

Your Treasurer keeps track of money and costs.

More Team Members:

You might have additional team members like product makers, sellers and customer service.

Match team member skills to team positions. For example, a Treasurer should be good at math.

Your team members can do more than one job.

Make your StoryTree® Business Plan:

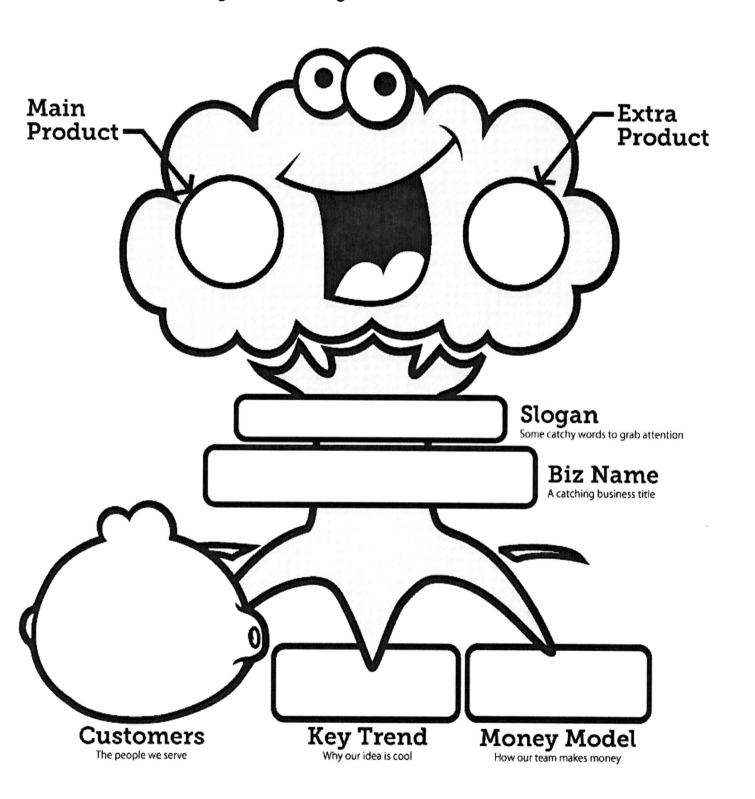

Main Product

Extra Product

Slogan
Some catchy words to grab attention

Biz Name
A catching business title

Customers
The people we serve

Key Trend
Why our idea is cool

Money Model
How our team makes money

© 2015, BizGym. All Rights Reserved. Provided courtesy BizGym.com, the entrepreneur's growth app

Draw Your Store:

Shade Tent? Sign Above? Logo? Slogan?

Menu

Outdoor
Wind
Weights

Order, Payment & Pickup Process?   Product Displays?

Table Top?   Table Skirt?   Uniforms?

TIP! Make signs easy to read from far away. If potential customers know what you're selling, there's more chance they'll come and shop.

11. Supply Your Store

List things needed:

Signs & Decorations

Overhead signs, table tops, table skirts, uniforms, menus, pricing.

_____

_____

_____

_____

_____

Equipment & Gear

Tables, chairs, tent (and weights if using a tent), product-making items, ties, tape.

_____

_____

_____

_____

Business Items

Cash box, pens, paper, receipts, etc.

_____

_____

_____

_____

Safety Items

First-aid kit, fire extinguisher, etc.

_____

_____

_____

_____

Always check with government agencies for health, business and other regulations and laws.

Involve your school, family & friends to get more sales!

Do a Budget:

1. Income: Estimate your main products, extras, tips and donations.

2. Sales Tax: Take a field trip to your local city business department for sales tax and business information.

3. Expenses: Estimate costs for everything you'll need. When you buy things, save the receipts so you can prove to the tax people that you spent money.

4. Income Tax: Ask your local city business department on how to pay taxes. You may have your parents do it with their taxes.

INCOME	$ Amount	
Main Produsts: (_____ products X $_____/product)		
Extra Products: (_____ extras X $_____ /extra)		
Tips & Donations		
Gross Income (add amounts above):		
Sales Tax (ask your City Business Department)		
Net Income (Gross Income minus Sales Tax):		

EXPENSES	$ Amount	
Total Expenses:		

NET PROFIT (Net Income minus Total Expenses)

Income Tax (ask your City Business Department)

AFTER TAX PROFIT (Net Profit minus Income Tax) $

13. Make a Contract

Agree on How to Share Profits:

Write in the name of your business and agreement date.

Write in names of team members and how much each gets.

Share Profits!
Consider giving some of your profits to a worthy cause like a charity or an investor like your parents.

All team members should sign and date this agreement.

This form is only an exercise. Take this to a lawyer to have an official agreement written.

AGREEMENT

THIS AGREEMENT for (business name) _____

made (date)_____ between the Members listed below is to

share After Tax Profits as follows:

Team Member Names	Profit Share
_____	_____%
_____	_____%
_____	_____%
_____	_____%
_____	_____%

Other Profit Share Members

_____	_____%
_____	_____%
_____	_____%

Total: 100%

WE THE MEMBERS, agree to the above terms.

Member Name	Signature	Date
_____	_____	_____
_____	_____	_____
_____	_____	_____
_____	_____	_____
_____	_____	_____

14. Plan Your Marketing

List how you'll get the word out:

Partners
Your family, companies or a charity might help.

_____

_____

_____

_____

_____

Invitations
Who should you tell about your business?

_____

_____

_____

_____

_____

Advertisements
How about flyers or team business cards?

_____

_____

_____

_____

Coupons
May be give discounts?

_____

_____

_____

_____

TIP: The more people that know and care about your business, the more you'll sell!

Tell the story of your business:
(make it entertaining with a song, poem, dance or skit)

TIP! Use your best skills and don't be afraid to be dramatic or silly!

Grabber: Start with something that makes people sit up and take notice!

Secret Sauce: Show what makes your product special, different and amazing.

How to Buy: Tell people what you want them to do. In business, if you ask, they'll buy more.

Words (What We'll Say)	**Action** (What We'll Do)
The Grabber:	
Your "Secret Sauce":	
How to Buy:	

Kid-preneurs are often interviewed by newspaper and TV reporters. Be ready with 3 big story ideas:

TV TIP! Turn on your smile during the introduction. Then just talk to the reporter and don't look at the camera.

Radio TIP! If they can't hear you, they won't get your story. So get close to the mic and speak up!

TV, Radio & Print TIP! Choose 3 important points things to say about your story. These may include your product, how you're selling, who you help, why what you're doing is important, or you might thank anyone who helped you get started. Be sure to tell them how they can buy your products.

1. Our business idea is...

2. We want to help (a charity or audience)...

3. Buy from us at...

As a kid-preneur, like any other business, you must obey business laws and share in the cost of community services like police and fire fighters.

Take a City Hall
Field Trip!

Visit your local city business department to get required permits and learn how to run a legal business.

Business Department

Business License

Sales & Income Tax

Insurance

Health Department

Health Permit

Food Safety

Too Much to Handle?

If you can't get permits or can't figure out how to pay for taxes and insurance, get an organization to do a Lemonade Alley near you!

See LemonadeAlley.com

What permits are required?

_____

_____

_____

What payments & taxes?

_____

_____

_____

Any business tips for kids?

_____

_____

_____

Heath Department Questions

What permits are required?

_____

_____

_____

Any regulations?

_____

_____

_____

Any food safety tips for kids?

_____

_____

_____

 Good Luck with Your Biz!

CPSIA information can be obtained at www.ICGtesting.com
Printed in the USA
LVOW09s2156180816

501000LV00013B/108/P